Vasco da Gama

Kristin Petrie

ABDO
Publishing Company

visit us at
www.abdopublishing.com

Published by ABDO Publishing Company, 8000 West 78th Street, Edina, Minnesota 55439.
Copyright © 2004 by Abdo Consulting Group, Inc. International copyrights reserved in all
countries. No part of this book may be reproduced in any form without written permission from
the publisher.

Printed in the United States of America, North Mankato, Minnesota.
012004 052013
Cover Photos: Corbis
Interior Photos: Corbis pp. 5, 7, 9, 11, 13, 17, 19, 20, 23, 25, 26, 27, 29; North Wind pp. 21, 24

Series Coordinator: Stephanie Hedlund
Editors: Kate A. Conley, Kristin Van Cleaf
Art Direction & Cover Design: Neil Klinepier
Interior Design & Maps: Dave Bullen

Library of Congress Cataloging-in-Publication Data

Petrie, Kristin, 1970-
    Vasco da Gama / Kristin Petrie.
        p. cm. -- (Explorers)
    Includes index.
    Summary: Describes the fifteenth century voyages taken by Portuguese explorer Vasco da
Gama, who furthered his nation's power by expanding trade routes to India.
    ISBN 1-59197-603-0
    1. Gama, Vasco da, 1469-1524--Juvenile literature. 2. Explorers--Portugal--Biography--
Juvenile literature. 3. Discoveries in geography--Portuguese--Juvenile literature. [1. Gama,
Vasco da, 1469-1524. 2. Explorers.] I. Title.

G286.G2P46 2004
910'.92--dc22
    [B]
                                                                    2003062924

Contents

Vasco da Gama

The respected title Admiral of the Sea of India was given to Vasco da Gama. In 1499, this Portuguese explorer accomplished what many men before him had only hoped to do. He opened a new route to the riches of Asia.

Gold, spices, and other Eastern goods were valuable in Europe in the 1400s. However, it was expensive and difficult to transport these items. So, many countries were trying to find a better route to the East.

Da Gama sailed about 27,000 miles (43,500 km) on his search. This voyage was nearly four times as long as Christopher Columbus's crossing to North and South America!

Da Gama became the first European to find an ocean trading route to India. He did this by sailing around the southern tip of Africa and then northeast to Asia. Portugal celebrated his accomplishment. In fact, every European country benefited from it.

1451	1485
Christopher Columbus born	Hernán Cortés born

1450	1460	1491
John Cabot born	Vasco da Gama born	Jacques Cartier born

Vasco da Gama

1492
Columbus's first voyage west for Spain

1496
Cabot's first voyage for England

1493
Columbus's second voyage, attempted to colonize Hispaniola

Early Life

Vasco da Gama was born around 1460 in the port town of Sines, Portugal. Vasco's parents were Isabel Sodré and Estevão da Gama. They were of noble **heritage**. Estevão was the governor of Sines and in service to Portugal's king John II. Vasco had at least two brothers.

Very little is known about Vasco's childhood. Being the son of a nobleman, Vasco most likely attended school. Children at that time studied reading, writing, and art. And young boys such as Vasco were probably influenced by tales of the sea, exploration, and discovery.

Vasco was Estevão and Isabel's third child, so he would not inherit his father's wealth. Vasco had to make his own fortune. He is said to have learned mathematics and navigation as a young man. This led him to become a soldier and **mariner**.

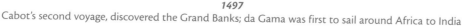

1497
Cabot's second voyage, discovered the Grand Banks; da Gama was first to sail around Africa to India

1496 or 1497
Hernando de Soto born

1498
Cabot's third voyage, may have died; Columbus's third voyage

Would You?

Would you have chosen to be an explorer? What other career options do you think Vasco da Gama had?

Sines is on Portugal's Atlantic coast.

1502
Columbus's fourth voyage; da Gama's second voyage

1504
Cortés sailed to the West Indies

1506
Columbus died

The Assignment

While Vasco was growing up, Portugal's rulers wanted to find a direct route to Asia. They hoped to establish trade with the countries of the East. They sent many explorers into **uncharted** waters.

In 1488, Portuguese explorer Bartolomeu Dias had made it as far as the eastern shore of southern Africa. Next, King John II chose Vasco's father to search for a sea route. Estevão was commanded to continue on from Dias's farthest landing point until he reached India.

Estevão, however, died while planning the voyage. The assignment was handed down to his son, Vasco. By that time, Vasco had become a soldier. He had earned a good reputation while defending Portugal's southernmost colonies from the French.

1511
Cortés helped take over Cuba

1510
Francisco Vásquez de Coronado born

1514
De Soto went to the New World

In 1487, Bartolomeu Dias began his journey to find a sea route to India. Dias made it as far as Rio de Infante, today's Great Fish River, before turning back.

The Departure

Da Gama set sail from Lisbon, Portugal, on July 8, 1497. He had 170 crew members to sail his ships. Many of the men were convicts. They were forced to do the most **dangerous** jobs.

Bartolomeu Dias also joined the voyage. Dias did not intend to make the entire trip, however. He would remain at São Jorge da Mina in what is now Ghana. There, Dias was to govern a new settlement.

Captain da Gama commanded the **fleet** of four ships from his **flagship**, the *São Gabriel*. Da Gama's older brother, Paulo, was in charge of the *São Rafael*. The *Berrio* was captained by Nicolao Coelho. A fourth ship carried supplies for the long journey.

1524
Da Gama's third voyage, died in Cochin, India

1519–1521
Cortés conquered the Aztec Empire and claimed Mexico for Spain

1532
De Soto helped attack the Inca Empire

Would You?

Would you trust convicts to sail your ships? Why do you think da Gama had convicts as crew members?

This drawing from the 1500s shows Lisbon, Portugal.

Around Africa

The **fleet** stopped briefly in the Cape Verde Islands. Then, it sailed south along Africa's coast. Next, da Gama turned the ships into the open sea.

Da Gama had a plan. He would sail far into the Atlantic to catch the westerly winds. The winds would help the ships sail farther south with more speed. They would round the tip of Africa in less time than if they followed the shore.

Da Gama put his plan into action. The fleet sailed to the middle of the ocean. Then, da Gama turned it back toward Africa. Nearly 100 days passed before the crew sighted land. Fresh food grew scarce, so many crew members became ill with **scurvy**.

The crew finally sighted the coast of Africa on November 1, 1497. Da Gama's plan, however, had not worked perfectly. The ships still had many miles to sail to reach the southern tip of the continent.

1533
De Soto helped take over Cuzco

1534
Cartier's first voyage for France

1535
Cartier's second voyage

1539–1542
De Soto explored La Florida

Da Gama's crew rounded the Cape of Good Hope on November 22. Three days later, the ships reached Mossel Bay on Africa's east coast. The crew marked their first landing with a stone pillar. Da Gama no longer needed the supply ship, so he had it destroyed. Then the remaining ships continued.

Bartolomeu Dias named the southernmost tip of Africa the Cape of Good Hope.

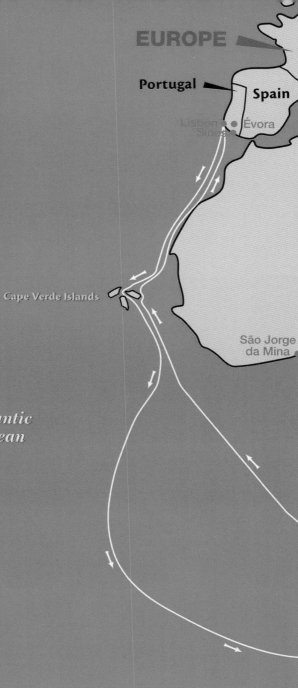

The Journey of Vasco da Gama

1497 TO 1499 →

EUROPE

Portugal
Spain

Lisbon
Sines
Évora

Cape Verde Islands

São Jorge
da Mina

*Atlantic
Ocean*

Brazil

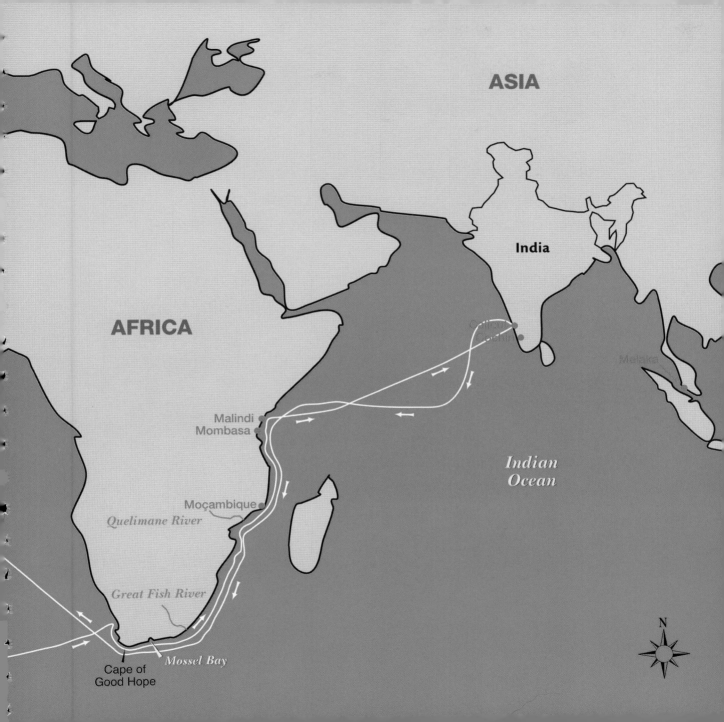

ASIA

India

AFRICA

Calicut
Cochin

Melaka

Malindi
Mombasa

Indian
Ocean

Moçambique

Quelimane River

Great Fish River

Mossel Bay

Cape of
Good Hope

N

Uncharted Waters

In the middle of December, the expedition passed another stone pillar. It was near the Great Fish River. This pillar marked the farthest point of Dias's voyage, and of Portuguese exploration.

The ships continued north along Africa's east coast. Strong currents made traveling slow and difficult. Many sailors again became sick with **scurvy**. At the Quelimane River, the crew took a month-long break. They repaired the ships and found fresh food.

Farther up the coast, the **fleet** stopped at the ports of Moçambique and Mombasa. **Muslims** in these cities had already established trade with India. The crew was thrilled with their first sight of Eastern goods. Fearing competition in their market, however, the Muslims refused to trade.

The Portuguese were welcomed at their next stop, however. The people of Malindi competed with the

Muslims of Moçambique and Mombasa. They welcomed the Portuguese traders as **allies**. They also provided da Gama with an Arab pilot for the **dangerous** Indian Ocean crossing.

The shore near Mombasa

1547
Cortés died

1557
Cartier died

1542
Coronado returned to New Spain; de Soto died

1554
Coronado died

1566
Drake's first voyage to the New World

India!

The **fleet** arrived in Calicut, India, on May 20, 1498. The sea route to the riches of Asia was complete! The landing marked the first European arrival in India by sea. Calicut was the principal market for trading Indian goods. Precious stones, pearls, and spices were plentiful.

At first, the Portuguese were well received by the Hindu ruler. The **Zamorin** was insulted, however, when he saw the items da Gama brought to trade. They were of little value compared to the Eastern treasures.

Da Gama was unable to establish a trading post. To make matters worse, the Zamorin demanded he pay a huge tax. Da Gama was furious and refused to pay! Instead, at the end of August 1498, the crew took five **hostages** and left Calicut.

1567
Drake's second voyage

1577
Drake began a worldwide voyage, was first Englishman to sail the Pacific Ocean

1570 and 1572
Drake terrorized the Spanish in the New World

Would You?

Would you pay the tax the Zamorin demanded? What goods do you think the Zamorin would have wanted?

Da Gama and the Zamorin discuss trade in Calicut.

Homeward

The **fleet** once again sailed into the Indian Ocean. Months later, they were back in the port of Malindi. It had been a difficult voyage and many of the sailors had died.

There weren't enough healthy crew members left to sail all three ships. So, da Gama ordered them to destroy the *São Rafael*. The crew was split between the two remaining ships.

This cross marks da Gama's landing near Malindi.

Da Gama and his crew then sailed south. They reached the Cape of Good Hope in March 1499. Six months later, da Gama reached Lisbon, Portugal.

1588
Drake helped England win the Battle of Gravelines against Spain's Invincible Armada

1581
Drake knighted by Queen Elizabeth I

1596
Drake died

More than two years had passed since the voyage began. Da Gama returned with one-third of his crew and half of his ships. And, he only had a small sample of the treasures they had found.

The Portuguese celebrated da Gama's return to Lisbon.

1728
James Cook born

1765
Boone journeyed to Florida

1768
Cook sailed for Tahiti

1734
Daniel Boone born

1767
Boone explored Kentucky

Admiral

Despite da Gama's setbacks, the voyage was a success! Vasco da Gama had discovered the first sea route from Western Europe to India. This would create a new method of trade, where no **middleman** profited. Portugal would soon have the upper hand in selling Eastern goods to all of Europe.

Da Gama was a hero. Portugal's king Manuel I awarded him a **pension** and a house. Da Gama was also named Admiral of the Sea of India.

The Portuguese quickly planned another voyage to India. This time, they sent a **fleet** of 13 vessels. Da Gama remained in Portugal, while Pedro Álvars Cabral led the expedition.

Captain Cabral also met with resistance when he reached Calicut, India. However, he established trading posts at another port called Cochin. Cabral returned to Portugal in 1501 with four ships loaded with valuable spices.

During da Gama's time in Portugal, he met a noblewoman. Vasco da Gama and Caterina de Ataíde were married around 1500. Over time, the couple had six sons.

On his way to India, Pedro Álvars Cabral sailed farther west than da Gama had. Cabral landed in Brazil, claimed this land for Portugal, and then continued on to India.

PEDRO ALVARES CABRAL

1778
Cook became the first European to record Hawaiian Islands; Boone captured by Shawnee

1775
Boone cut the Wilderness Road from Virginia to Kentucky

1779
Cook died

Revenge

Following Cabral's return, da Gama was granted another voyage to India. The expedition was sent to expand on the trade Cabral had established. Da Gama also had revenge on his mind.

Vasco da Gama

In February 1502, da Gama set sail with a large **fleet**. The 20 ships were well armed. Da Gama planned to force his way into the trading market.

The expedition soon reached Calicut. The **Zamorin** was willing to sign a trade agreement. However, da Gama insisted that the leader **banish** the **Muslims**. He wanted a **monopoly** over trade. This

1813
John C. Frémont born

1842
Frémont's first independent surveying mission

1820
Boone died

Spices from India were part of da Gama's trade agreement with the Zamorin.

would make Portugal wealthy and repay the **Muslims** for their opposition in 1498.

To show his power, da Gama killed many innocent Indians and Muslims. Eventually, the Portuguese took over the city of Calicut. This act was extremely profitable and secured Portuguese trading in the East Indies.

More Honors

Da Gama returned to Lisbon in 1503. Unlike his first voyage, this time da Gama brought back many treasures. Once again, he was a hero.

Da Gama retired after his return. He spent the following 20 years in Évora, Portugal. The Portuguese empire continued to expand in the East.

In 1519, da Gama was made **count** of Vidigueira, a region in Portugal. This entitled him to collect taxes and rent from two Portuguese towns. This income and the profitable trade voyages made da Gama a wealthy man.

Count Vasco da Gama

1856
Frémont ran for president of the United States but lost

1845-1846
Frémont explored the Great Basin and the Pacific Coast, fought in the Mexican War

1890
Frémont died

Would You?

Would you be able to retire after having had so many adventures? Do you think da Gama enjoyed his time in Portugal?

Today, Évora is an agricultural trading center.

1910
Jacques Cousteau born

1951
Cousteau's first expedition in the Red Sea

1942
Cousteau and Gagnan developed the Aqua-Lung for diving

Later Years

Many years later, Portugal's king John III feared a loss of control in India. He appointed da Gama the Portuguese **viceroy** there. So, da Gama returned to the sea.

Da Gama embarked on his final voyage to India in 1524. He arrived in Goa in September and immediately set to work. Da Gama attempted to reverse the damage done by the viceroys before him.

Soon after da Gama assumed control, he became ill. Vasco da Gama died in Cochin, India, on December 24, 1524. His remains were taken back to Portugal in 1538.

After da Gama's death, Portugal's empire continued to grow. Trade was established in Melaka, the most important city in the East Indies. Following this, the Portuguese pushed on to China.

Vasco da Gama's accomplishments had opened Europe's door to the East. Other European countries soon followed Portugal's example.

1997
Cousteau died

1974
Cousteau formed the Cousteau Society to protect marine life

This statue of da Gama stands in his hometown of Sines, Portugal.

DOM VASCO DA GAMA
1469 - 1524

DESCOBRIDOR E ALMIRANTE DO MAR DA INDIA
1º CONDE DA VIDIGUEIRA
VICE - REI DA INDIA

"...AQUELLE ILLUSTRE GAMA
QUE PARA SI DE ENEAS TOMA A FAMA."
CAMÕES, LUS, I - 12

Glossary

allies - people or countries that agree to help each other in times of need.

banish - to drive out or officially require someone to leave and never return.

count - a noble who was the governor of a county.

dangerous - able or likely to cause injury or harm.

flagship - the ship that carries the officer in command of a fleet or squadron and displays his flag.

fleet - a group of ships under one command.

heritage - the handing down of something from one generation to the next.

hostage - a person held captive by another person or group in order to make a deal with authorities.

mariner - a person who is involved with the navigation of a ship.

middleman - someone who buys goods from the producer and then sells them to a retailer or directly to the consumer.

monopoly - the complete control of a product, service, or industry.

Muslim - a person who follows Islam. Islam is a religion based on the teachings of the prophet Muhammad as they appear in the Koran.

pension - money for people to live on after they retire.

scurvy - a fatal disease caused by lack of vitamin C.

uncharted - something that is unknown and therefore has not been recorded on a map, chart, or plan.

viceroy - a governor who acts as the representative of a king or queen.

Zamorin - the title of the Hindu ruler of Calicut during the 1400s and 1500s.

Saying It

Bartolomeu Dias - bahr-too-loo-MAYUH DEE-uhsh
Cochin - koh-CHIHN
Moçambique - moo-suhm-BEE-kuh
Mossel Bay - MAW-suhl BAY
Quelimane - kuh-lee-MAH-nuh
Vidigueira - vee-dee-GAY-rah

Web Sites

To learn more about Vasco da Gama, visit ABDO Publishing Company on the World Wide Web at **www.abdopublishing.com**. Web sites about Vasco da Gama are featured on our Book Links page. These links are routinely monitored and updated to provide the most current information available.

Index